TOPAZ

TOPAZ

BRIAN KOMEI DEMPSTER

four way books
tribeca

In memory of my grandparents, Archbishop Nitten Ishida and Chiyoko Saito Ishida,

and my uncles, Hidemaro, Kunimaro, and Kibimaro Ishida

Please direct all inquiries to:
Editorial Office
Four Way Books
POB 535, Village Station
New York, NY 10014
www.fourwaybooks.com

Library of Congress Cataloging-in-Publication Data

Dempster, Brian Komei, date
[Poems. Selections]
Topaz : poems / by Brian Komei Dempster.
pages cm
Includes bibliographical references.
ISBN 978-1-935536-33-8 (alk. paper)
I. Title.
PS3604.E4755T67 2013
811'.6--dc23
                                    2013004423

This book is manufactured in the United States of America and printed on acid-free paper.

Four Way Books is a not-for-profit literary press. We are grateful for the assistance
we receive from individual donors, public arts agencies, and private foundations.

NATIONAL
ENDOWMENT
FOR THE ARTS

This publication is made possible with public funds from the National Endowment for the Arts

State of the Arts

NYSCA

and from the New York State Council on the Arts, a state agency

[clmp]

We are a proud member
of the Council of Literary Magazines and Presses.

Distributed by University Press of New England
One Court Street, Lebanon, NH 03766

TABLE OF CONTENTS

TOPAZ

I am the prism

    refracting

your prison.

    My ancestors,

the jewels

    set in sand.

Through facets

    I etch memory.

From crystal

    my lines

are cut.

CROSSING

No turning back. Deep in the Utah desert now, having left one home
    to return to the temple of my grandfather. I press the pedal
        hard. Long behind me, civilization's last sign—a bent post
            and a wooden board: *No food or gas for 200 miles.* The tank

        needling below half-full, I smoke Camels to soothe
    my worry. Is this where it happened? What's left out there of Topaz
in the simmering heat? On quartzed asphalt I rush

        past salt beds, squint at the horizon for the desert's edge: a lone
          tower, a flattened barrack, some sign of Topaz—the camp
             where my mother, her family, were imprisoned. As I speed
               by shrub cactus, the thought of it feels too near,

        too close. The engine steams. The radiator
      hisses. Gusts gather, wind pushes my Civic side
    to side, and I grip the steering wheel, strain to see

through a windshield smeared with yellow jacket wings, blood
    of mosquitoes. If I can find it, how much can
        I really know? Were sandstorms soft as dreams or stinging
           like nettles? Who held my mother when the wind whipped

            beige handfuls at her baby cheeks? Was the sand tinged
        with beige or orange from oxidized mesas? *I don't remember*
    my mother's answer to everything. High on coffee

and nicotine, I half-dream in waves of heat: summon ghosts
from the canyon beyond thin lines of barbed wire. Our name
Ishida. *Ishi* means stone, *da* the field. We were gemstones
strewn in the wasteland. Only three days

and one thousand miles to go before I reach
San Francisco, the church where my mother was born
and torn away. Maybe Topaz in the desert was long

gone, but it lingered in letters, photos, fragments
of stories. My mother's room now mine, the bed pulled blank
with ironed sheets, a desk set with pen and paper. Here
I would come to understand.

EIGHTFOLD CHANT

Church of broken toasters and singed fuses,
church of the dripping roof and chipped chimney stack,
of the flooded garage and its split door,

gas-hissing pipes and sibilant water heaters,
church of piss-poor light and shaky ladders
where I unchoke windows and dislodge chopsticks

from pipes, smooth curled up wallpaper and key the locks,
fix clocks sticking or ticking with different times,
church where wings of dead flies drift like petals

from cobwebs, ghosts sift through floorboards
and the homeless sleep in compost, steeping like tea bags
pungent from the leaves' damp weight.

Church where I am summoned by the door's clatter of brass
to the brown-toothed vagrant who spreads open
her overcoat; to the chattering man who communes

with pines and brooms the stairs; to the bent, old Japanese woman
who forgets her keys, waits for me to twist the lock free
so she can scrub floors with Murphy wood soap

and a toothbrush, wobble atop a ladder and polish the two-ton bell.
On this path I am my uncle setting cubes of cheese into jaws
of traps, and my grandmother stirring peas into a pan of fried rice,

and my grandfather padding the halls in slippers and gloves,
the cold globes of his breath a string of prayer beads
weaving me, a mixed-blood grandson, into them.

SUGAR

I.

Sweet is my grandfather who leans forward
in his chair, squints at his plate.
With clasped hands, he carves
a sutra out of air. With a napkin,

I wipe the steam from his glasses.
Begin with this prayer. And if its chant
is sweet, then listen for it while he tastes
the blindness growing inside him like a field

of snow peas, the green which flickers
at the edges of his retinas. Between a row
of pods where he knelt, he held them
and snapped off the stems. One by one

they plinked his bucket of rust, so quiet,
the same quiet of my chopsticks
as their tips reach into the green accumulation,
pearl by pearl I lift to his mouth.

II.

Sweet jazz, I guess my ex-girlfriend
is *baby honey sweetheart*
each variation a saxophone moan
while our flesh met on top

of parking lots marked "Do Not Enter."
There are limits to a body *baby honey*
in bathroom stalls with flimsy locks, *sweetheart*
in love seats of theaters. If first love begins sweet

as improvisation, then let the ending change,
no longer her father's breath, tinged with *soju*
as he pulls her from my arms and shoves her
in the backseat. Let it change from the sound

of his spilling coins to the sapphire triangles
of her earrings, from the taste of burning tires
into oleanders, dahlias, their perfumed fragrance.
Let sugar dissolve the exhaust.

III.

Not sweet, but bitter gruel
mixed with a spoonful of sugar.
Sit next to my grandmother:
the rails of the bed containing her,

breath halts and flows in her river throat,
the IV feeds her body of dreams.
If I towel her damp bangs, she stares
back, absent. So I open the book

to its whispering of mahogany, cedar,
and hemlock. This sutra is sugar
as long as it bathes her with my syllables,
soothes her glottal stops. The clock

sips from its frayed cord.
I push the button that feeds her.
The minutes are turned pages
beneath the simple lamp on the simple stand.

IV.

Sweet is our dissolving.
The young woman I loved leans her weight
into an iron, steaming the wrinkles from muslin.
In his shop, her father folds each sheet

she finishes, her face moist from the sweat.
I still see her cheek pressing against the sealed window
of his car as he took her away. I will carry
tulips down a long hallway, and throw the petals

into a chamber of stone. Something is sweet
about the bones, my grandfather and grandmother
burning on the other side of a latched door.
I don't want desire but it overtakes me,

the way I move with her against her father's floor,
and afterwards clean up my hairs from his rug.
By the edge of the creek, there are words
about the dead. The way our palms hold onto sugar

and the wind lets it go as ash.

STORM BREAKS

Every war begins somewhere. The boundaries
are me: my face. smile. language. my job. No matter what I did

your father thought I was crossing him. Between
your apartment and mine, we stood a breath

apart, your mouth a border shutting out

gentler words. I grabbed you by the T-shirt
like a bag of rice, you pushed me back, a ball of heat

enveloping us. When a forest ignites, balding the hills,
who lit the match, who flung it into the bed

of pine needles? Out the accusations came, armed

like soldiers barring the way, backing me into your corner,
You never bring flowers to the house. You haven't even learned

to pronounce my parents' names. You don't ever bow
and speak to my father in Korean. And I, half-Japanese,

barely able to speak the first language of my own mother,

Fuck no, I don't understand. I kicked over
my bottle of Old English, making shards

and gold foam. *Not you. Not your father.* Cicada hum
through razed fields. Fists filled electric

from our earlier lovemaking. Clouds varicosed with lightning, close

to releasing. *I want him to say my name, speak to me
in English.* I ignored the siren's tornado warning. When your collar

ripped, I held on. Your face divided, one half
in lamplight, the other fluttering with diamond-shadows

of elm leaves. Over forty years ago. In Korea. A woman held

down. Her dress pulled up. A Japanese soldier inside. The soles
of our shoes sticky with liquor, crunching

on broken glass. What could I do? A great aunt.
A grandmother. Your father's mother? You wouldn't tell

me. The siren's next blare. My chest tightened. I looked

down at our feet, the tips of our shoes touched, squashing
the tuft of grass sprouting from the sidewalk's jagged

fault. Where was I? Who told your father? Did he tell you?
A man's grunts, a woman's screams. Static claws

the air, sounds become foreign. Sheaves

of barley, frozen soil. Rain falls into
asphalt's divide, our black hair damp, cicadas quieted. Beneath

elms, your ribs' gentle quaking, skies webbing us
with tangled light. When I look back through storm-fire,

we are huddled close, smoldering.

SHEER

How many men
        I don't know. If there were

handcuffs I've not
        been told. Seven decades later

they're invisible
        to me, and I to them.

Through chiffon drapes
        my grandfather peered back

at my grandmother.
        Her orange *kimono* wings rose,

fluttered away
        her children huddling

in peach silk quilts.
        December 1941. On their porch

did he bow his head
        in prayer or feigned deference

as he felt the light
        around him shift to pearl, then dark?

YOUR HANDS GUIDE ME THROUGH TRAINS

From the bridge we stare down at the track, searching
the arch, where rails curve out of darkness. You lift me
on your shoulders and we balance in white light, the dead center
approaching. The whistle blows, a rumble climbs
through the bones of your feet, through your legs and hands into mine,

your right hand clenches my right,
your left hand clenches my left,
if this were 1942, my hands would be the handle
of your suitcase and your purple book scripted
in prayer. Torn from family, you board a boxcar, snap open

your case, set your brush and ink to the right,
stones to the left, paint your own sea and coast
as the plains, grass, and ironwoods rattle by.
You dip the brush in each camp and each barrack,
fill the paper with kelp and jellyfish, pebbles and shells,

tape the sheets side by side. When it grows
dark, you draw tracks leading to the edge of the tide.
Asking for water, your hands unclasp and cling
to the wires as men rip the sash from your back.
A rifle butt knocks prayer loose from your throat.

But it is 1976, a Sunday like any other,
when you drape beads over my wrists and open
the Lotus Sutra on the bridge, anchor its pages with stones,
offer prayers as the train rushes under our feet,
our lungs flowering with soot and steam.

For years, I traveled to your hands, unrolled ocean scrolls
from your case. In barracks you'd held the brush, painting
your way out. By 1996 your brushstrokes fade, *washi* crumples
in my palms. Your fingers grip a cane, waver with chopsticks.
Soup, tea, and rice sprig your bib. I feed you, brush your teeth,

my right hand clenches your right, my left clenches your left,
I lower you in the chair, place your feet on the steel ledges.
Grandfather, can we run just once through the gravel, along silver rail,
watch flames curl off the faces of men smudged in coal?
Can you take me to Missoula and Fort Sill, wheels circling back

to Crystal City? We arrive at the church where you live, and I wheel you
past rows of empty chairs, drape the sash over your back, strike
a match, light sticks of incense. Your hands guide me
through the years like a black iron rope, into the orange glow,
a tunnel of smoke, pages returning us to the shores of our home.

—for Archbishop Nitten Ishida, 1901-1996

AT THE THRESHOLD

It's so hard
to forgive.
I brim with rage
at the way the men grab
your father
by the *kesa*
twist his chrysanthemum sash.
And upstairs
you, Mother, his infant daughter
who sleeps, as they lead him
from your church home
to the waiting car.

I FACTOR IN MY MOTHER'S DIVISION FROM HER FATHER WITH A SENTENCE WRITTEN BY LIEUTENANT GENERAL JOHN L. DEWITT IN 1942

Still unbalanced
    about why.

          The very fact that

    there were no facts, just imaginary signs:
My grandfather's coral prayer beads.

    His transistor radio he left glowing. His sons burning

leaves in their church backyard.
    Tall tomato plants pointing

        no sabotage

toward the east. Among thousands
    of suspected suspects:

Grandmother and her kitchen drawer

    of knives. Their daughters tuning into Imperial, twisting
the radio knob to catch the static. Though nothing

       has taken place

    except his wife's dress billows
into a flare. 1942. 2,592 guns.

1,458 radios. 2,014 cameras.

In the long
         division

                              to date is

Grandfather erased
         from my mother, her two-year-old face x-ed

behind barbed wire,

         a numbered tag
attached to her coat. Fabricated formulas

                  a disturbing

         tunnel to a storehouse of invisible guns and dynamite
where her father supposedly hides,

         when he's really trapped in an open desert far from his daughter

coughing in her steamer-trunk crib.
         These facts of her

                      and confirming indication

of me and this page swirl into a Topaz blur
    of over sixty years ago,

and the calculations storm with sand

    counting her out
and she wonders now

        that such action

    along with the vanished
scent of her father's breath and skin

    how her heart continues

to open
    and when it

        will be taken.

STEAMER TRUNK

You know us well,
     from Brendan teething in the church
to my mother's fenced-in thirst,
     from the possibility of chocolate
to the tinny taste of eel. Slow carrier

     of silver and sand,
from distance and troubled time
     to us and our son Brendan,
who, in unknown sympathy,
     wails on your lid

like his baby grandmother did
     in Topaz prison camp
for her absent father. Makeshift crib
     built by his gloved hands,
a wool blanket stapled as lining

     for your splintered wood skin,
she quieted in you,
     calming to cricket-song
beyond barbed wire, her body
     sheltered by you from the cold

that pushed through cracks
        of the barrack door. Strongbox
of only what we can carry,
        my wife Grace towels off Brendan,
and I set him down

        on his nursery floor, pry you
open with a crowbar. We unload
        your bent tinware and brittle-wicked candles
set for meals of *unagi*
        from jagged lids of dusty cans

on my mother's birthdays in Topaz,
        when her sisters Nori and Tae draped you
with wrinkled lilac silk.
        Barrack heirloom table
they squatted at, we sweep out

        and fill you with Brendan's ironed clothes
and toys, between sips of bottled milk
        he crawls up to touch your sides
we wipe clean, tugs at your latch, temple chest
        of rusted sweetness.

A CONVERSATION WITH MY MOTHER, RENKO, ABOUT THE JOURNEY
TO AND FROM TOPAZ PRISON CAMP IN A DREAM

A lotus is a lotus.
A train is a train.

No, this train is a lotus, this lotus is a train.

The petals are white swords.
The engine a head of steam.

No, petals are spumes of ash blooming from this train.

The bud opens to water.
The pistons drive with flame.

No, this train drives down the zone of the stem,
the petals fold back into a tunnel.

A lotus is a flower.

No, it is your cold body wrapped in cotton.
This bud is your lips muzzling milk
from your mother in the iron box.

A boxcar is a train.

No, your mother is this train, and her eyes are white cones
slicing mist in radiant columns. The boxcars slide
down the stem like drops of dark water.

You think I wanted to be this lotus,
I wanted to board this train?

No, the stem is not a lotus in mud.
You are buried knee-deep in a camp full of shit.
Your barrack is a box of panes and iron,
your camp a coal splitting with dust and plains.

The lotus may have been lost in the desert.
The desert may have been found in the train.

No, the train is a string of boxcars.
Each boxcar a chunk of dust I pluck from your stem.
Your stem is a mile of sharp, thistled wire.

I see a bulb sliding in you, my father.
Black steel ripping mist from tunnels. Your mother.
Steam and heat cleanse the walls. This is your lover.
A boy dripping with water is me, the son.

Mother, maybe steel thorns are milk, areolas rims
of light, the granite peak a triangle of hair,

. . . this soot is a flower,
your lungs a wisp of cinders,
your hair silver rail, your spine a track . . .

. . . veins are barracks, your knuckles
tar paper, this tower your throat,
this lotus your fist . . .

. . . your breast is my mouth, my tongue milk
your fingers white swords,
this stem your breath, it grew from flesh and dirt . . .

A lotus might not be a lotus.
A train might not be a train.

SICKNESS

That day I left my uncle Kibi, his lungs flushed in a barium rush,
I plunged my mother in ice. Derek and I rubbed
nine-volt batteries over our tongues and screwed the caps
off Mickey's. *Give her water* my father said
as he rubbed cubes over her chest and forehead and yanked

the plug. We drained the amber down our throats through a surgical tube,
whitewash running down my uncle's esophagus. At 101 she faced me
naked, arms shaking. I clawed through my father's dark bag,
jammed a Trojan in my pocket. He robed her dripping body,
snapped his trombone case. *Stay here. Take care of her.*

We hopped in Derek's Mustang, running reds and stops, her column
of mercury 103. *I'll be back soon. Mom, you need medicine.*
My head hanging out the window, I threw up and pulled
into Amber's driveway. The door opened and Christine led him
downstairs, Amber led me up, uncle Kibi shut into a room

marked "chemo." *Pull out* she said, *it doesn't feel good* driving
my finger *Please* . . . the phone rang, my father's backstage voice rolling
Where the fuck are you? 105 my mother bloating like a jellyfish,
106 the click of Derek's ignition, a string of red driving to Emergency.
Ruptured appendix the surgeon said. *Advanced lymphoma*

the test confirmed. Then a slick curve crushing Derek between steering
wheel and seat, a shattered bottle his mouth, Kibi breathing
through a tank marked "Oxygen." My father dressing her hip in gauze,
balancing her steel walker, Amber's mother pulling my wrapper
from the trash. *I want to come home* my uncle whispered

over the phone. *I can't see you anymore* Amber told me,
the cops slipping Derek's keys in a bag marked "Evidence."
Tumors sprouted like cauliflower against Kibi's lungs.
My voice spiraled through the cord *I want you to come back.*
My uncle thinning in critical, my mother released, Christine climbing

through my window, resting her drunk head on my stomach,
slurring *I miss him. I missed you* my father whispering upstairs,
rubbing her line of stitches as we hardened in Trojans. She on top
of me, he on top of her, Christine crying *Don't put anything on . . .*
my mother crying *Not too hard . . . the wound will open.*

TEMPLE BELL LESSON

Son, I am weighted.
    You are light.

Our ancestors imprisoned,
    outcast

in sand, swinging
    between scorching air

and the insult
    of blizzards.

Their skin bronzed
    and chilled

like brass,
    listen

to their sorrow
    ringing.

TRANSACTION

1992, my mother opened
     an envelope from the White House.
A decade before, Vincent Chin
     had swung open doors
of a Detroit strip club
     and slapped down a ten

for a beer. In Seattle,
     I tuck a crisp five
in the belt of a Jamaican dancer.
     Vincent and I, 2,000 miles apart,
thumbing through wads of cash:
     the checkered strobe

and women clenching poles,
     spiked heels scissor-kicked
in blinking indigo.
     $20,000 and an apology, signed
by the President. *They spelled*
     my name wrong she muttered. A white father

and son, lacquered
     in piston grease, fired
from the plant.
     My name's Francine
she whispers as she snaps
     my bill, swiveling her hips

to Motown. They swilled gins,
            Four years in the camps
my mother said, raising
            her check to the light.
Damn Jap
            they thought aloud

as Vincent downed
            a Miller. *I'll spend it on you,*
Loren, and your Dad she said.
            Francine does the splits
as I follow her hips.
            We'll split it

four ways. The father and son gulped
            flasks of whiskey.
My mother sealed
            the check in the envelope.
Behind cars the two crouched, clenching
            bats. When the song ends,

I search my pockets—pennies
            and nickels, stubs
and receipts. Vincent walked out,
            the cool oak opening his skull
like a piggy bank.
            My mother stuffed the money

in a safe. I crack
        my billfold. *Nothing can pay me back*
she said. Through emptied space
        I fumble.
Four years, coming back to our church—
        a broken

home. The father and son paid $3,000,
        3 years probation. In my denims
I pack my wallet
        and slide out *The Sands.*
My son was Chinese
        Vincent's mother wept.

They were provoked
        the judge said. My mother tore out
checks for tuition, *Nothing can take that away*
        she told us. I stumble
among years and models. She signed
        for a four-door

Honda Civic. *I don't regret*
        what we did the father said,
He had it coming said the son.
        Which car is mine? I wonder
in the dim lot. *Come again*
        Francine's voice echoes

as I unlock my Ford, swivel
      the key in the ignition.
I strap my seatbelt and palm
      my crotch, surge with
the electricity of lust, the rush
      of swinging a bat.

THE STRIP

after C.K. Williams

It was easy getting to that place,
        a row of halogen lamps arched above
the stretch of sidewalk Derek and I,
        16, drove past in his Mustang, circled them,

the hookers slinky in their mini dresses
        and high heels. At corners we paused,
undressed them, my palms sweaty
        as they broke into singles, gathered

in pairs, ducking into doorways
        or alleys when a squad car cruised by.
Back and forth, we passed a paper bag
        with a can of Foster's in it,

an unguent making me, at first, shiver,
        then cooling me into the moment
when we coupled with them. If I stay
        in one place, only look back,

this story begins with Derek's hand
        firm on the wheel while I search
the rearview mirror for cops,
        the streets leading us to sex.

Or I could look ahead for a sign,
          to the night I open the door
to our apartment, step back from
          the olive fold-out where Derek licks

the earlobe of his friend with sapphire eyes
          and an auburn beard, a weekend guest
he calls Steve. Or I could travel further,
          up the road where I drive Derek,

turn the slick pages of *Life* at a curb's red zone
          while he gets tested for his cough, the mucus
drying in tissues I lift from our carpet
          with plastic bags over my hands.

Or I could go to the end,
          when I uncrumple the slip of paper
with the number of his anonymous test
          and invent words the nurse said.

But I need to begin at the strip
          where signs are neon pearls cast
on the black hood of the car,
          where we find ourselves blinded

by an alley, unable to turn
        from the woman alone and swaying
beneath a streetlight, up close
        just a girl shivering.

I shuddered at the braces
        on her teeth, the dark circles under
her eyes, her face aged by the tint
        of powder and rouge.

It was Derek who climbed out,
        steered her reins of stringy hair
until he drove through her with his eyes closed,
        deep into anywhere, letting me see.

ADMISSION

There's a threshold I won't step over, men strolling hand in hand
    into a room embalmed

with disco and dry ice. Their diaphanous shapes
                hovering, I turn the key

    in the deadbolt of our family church, brush dust

from Buddha's black skin. Placing my hand
    on Grace's belly while she hums

Cantonese to the thump of our new heart
            beating, I picture scrubbing

    a man's back, tasting his words

as he wakes up. My admission
    glitters, knife-like, sways with the men

under the globe of mirrors, frays the cord
            between me, my wife Grace, and Brendan,

    our unborn son. The thought of my desire mixes

with steam and the private saltwater
    he alone breathes as I press out

the chaos in every rumple, divide
                the clothes still warm,

    into our closets, build the crib

from screws and slats.
        When we peel off

our jeans, her body is all entrances, the salt
                between her legs indiscernible

    from birth and mist rising

from damp T-shirts of strobe-lit men
      whirling on flashing tiles. Caught

between discovering the club's new sweat
             or staying home to iron it out, I clear

    a path with tongue against flesh, pair

father and mother, cunt
    and cock, my lust for Grace

complicated by how her taupe, freckled skin
             is Chinese and by how I, too, admire

the view from behind, this art of hers

to receive me face-down
    in the pillow. A straight road forks

into hip clubs of funk beats
        with men's tight backsides

    in black chaps. A man admits men

at the door, and I watch
    myself enter, the simple

thrusts, the sonogram's fleshy stub, the back
        and forth of Grace's *Oh*

    and my dirty talk, our tones

melding into
    the Lotus Sutra's pitched vowels,

Namu Myōhō Renge Kyō
        We begin.

CHANDELIER

Crystals break light into desert stars, my grandparents skies
     apart, deemed traitorous. How do
I clear them? Seven diamond-spears

          stream down, twist above. Who took
     the missing eighth? Our absence captured by one glassless string.
     Ceiling latticed with leaf-shadow,

drops silver as blades of strangers who carved initials
     into the banister, scattered oak flakes
on the stairs. Everywhere under guard, Grandfather whittled

          scrap wood into shapes. Rainbowed conduits
     my family left behind, Grace and I reshape the future, imagine
     touching our son Brendan's shiny scar—

will his electric brain be quieted? I ride the black sea of her hair
     falling over my shoulders, the night-tide
of Brendan's breath. A truck rumbles outside, makes glass

          on glass magic. Mirrored doors of trains
     cargoing my grandfather, his face tinted by floodlit torches.
     The noon's sun magnifies, shocking

his skin. On barrack steps, he shaved and sanded
     a carp figurine for his wife trapped
with their five children in Topaz—dull and barren

jewel. In bed Grace clings to me,
and I wait for Brendan's next exhale. Inside prisms,
our son reflects us all.

CAMP LETTERS

They open like lotuses
        in a water sky. In the lost strips
of snipped lines, I feel war's incision,

the censor's urge to cut out
        chunks of my grandparents' ink-steeped love.
Yet their voices stay bold,

rustle with uprisings, leave Grandfather's questions
        to Grandmother—*Do the children have enough
clothes and toys?*—stamps peeling

back, once bitter on their tongues,
        stiff with the memory of deserts
flecked with burdock and cholla,

miles of thorny wire between
        them, sweet with the chocolate he sends
to his wife, daughters, and sons.

In margins is the children's cure
        for missing this temple house: inscriptions
of a bridge trellised in fog, their garden

of bougainvillea, stick figures
        of them holding hands on the porch
lined with aster and sage.

Now nightfall blackens
the attic and dusk weans me
from the milk of their ink.

WINTER LETTER TO SAN FRANCISCO

February 19, 1942

Dear Chiyoko,

Your dress billows like tar paper, the fence
pinning loose squares of silk. I
start this letter through wire, write
you a trail of diamond husks and underbrush,
look for you across the desert. But my room
is four walls and rotting planks. Drops

of rain fall through cracks the way we did: Drop
your life, board a freight, spend years behind a fence.
The night they dragged me from our church, the upstairs room
clung to me: there, I had rubbed oil into your back, and your eyes
closed to my hands. I brushed
my tongue between your breasts and here I write

to you of burial, an old friend. Right
outside the barrack, a line of us dropped
back against the wall. Oshima-san ran, floodlights brushing
his face gold. He climbed the fence
until chrome plugs wilted him in the eye
of the light, back slapping the ice shadows. Make room

44

in your day to burn jasmine, gather our kids in one room
to pray. I hear rumors of soldiers' hands on Oshima's wife. Right
before the shot, I retreated into your eyes,
the shade of your hair. Now the roof laves me with drops.
Did this begin with prison? Did the kids fix our fence?
Break the records, fold the flag, throw my brushes

in a trunk. I wish you knew this sky—the clouds brush
a ceiling, mesa and cliff arching into a room.
Hawks land on the fence,
spread their wings into dusk—the sun writes
lines in quartz as the horizon falls. Drop
what you're doing, watch the sky with me. I

dream of painting you in the boards, dabbing in eyes,
stroking the arc of your hips with my brush.
You step out of ink, the cage drops
away, we rise from a bath, misting, in a room
in another country, an imagined town, where I write
the script of a history, in a courtyard with no fence.

Tonight the winds lift as I brush
your hair, drops of plum ink filling the room
in curves, my right hand stroking you through the fence.

SPRING REPLY TO INTERNMENT CAMP, LOCATION UNKNOWN

March 19, 1942

Dear Nitten,

I look deep, see the stroke of your brush, waves growing
into canvas. With each horsehair sweep, you shape
a shore of starfish and urchin, a luminous ocean.
I write you into haiku, gulls gliding home
through fog, fluttering against our church windows.
You rattle the mailbox and approach our door,

wind clicking the brass knocker. Slamming doors,
the children pause in the hall, wait for your glassed face to grow
beyond the photograph. Behind a train window
they frame you, imagine your trip from prison, back to us. The beacon shapes
an eyelet in the fog. I link lines, straight as rails, to bring you home.
Miles away you paint whitecaps soft, and I hold Renko by the ocean.

Today, the girls molded sand while Renko cooed *bird . . . mama . . . ocean . . .*
pointed at gulls swooping through clouds like doors,
landing on castles, white plumes giving her *papa . . . home . . .*
A soft giggle when she touched a feather. *Don't cry, you won't grow
up without papa.* The boys shape
your absence into games with bats, the crack of our altar window

followed by the sprinkle of glass, the window
I pick up, piece by piece. Maybe they mock the ocean,
shards of Pearl Harbor hissing into the tide. How do we shape
such fire? We haven't forgotten prayer. Like doors,
the covers parting open, your sutras growing
like lotuses from our throats. For now, our kids savor home

in their teeth, wrappers peeled from chocolates you send home.
How long will we be here safe, the children crouching behind windows,
stringing their wrists with beads, praying for your envelopes. Renko grows
warm inside the bear-clawed tub, its ocean
of lavender bubbles where she floats on a door
of water, and I memorize her shape

for you, unwrap your paintings we hid in rafters. With syllables I shape
locked gates into openings you could walk through, homeward
to Renko and us, your arms lifting her from me and through the door,
lowering her into her crib. At every window
I wonder if you find rain, miss the ocean
of winged figures inside my poems where you grow.

Shapes dissolve, and words become our windows.
We go home in envelopes, the ocean rolling us into each other.
These letters widen doorways, let us grow.

NORIKO FRAGMENTS

—Topaz, 1943

Thanks Papa

    for the chocolate.

  I opened it.

    Do you want some?

It's melted.

  I hid the silver paper.

Mama says

    stay far

  from the fence.

MY QUESTIONS TO OBACHAN, HER ANSWERS

In barracks, Grandma, the dust chafed your lips?
Men gathered for poker, the women for bridge.

And guards, rifles, the sweep of sleek black boots?
The girls cut out dolls, ripped paper into skirts.

Or towers, gleaming, loaded with silver barrels?
The copperheads slid through the sand and thistle.

My mother, newborn, draining your milk?
The hides snagged the fence, wires molting with snake.

And Grandpa, prairies east, did he send mail?
Boys slit the throats, white venom dripped from scales.

Did your son answer "yes," gut Nazis in France?
They batted rocks and coal through the fence.

Why give me sticks and skirts, these dolls and fangs?
Dusk rose like a flag, the red sun of Japan.

Atomic blasts across seas, trains steaming home?
I clouded a mirror, plucked hair from my comb.

Your church in Japantown, gold arch of the Bay?
I read my husband's words: "Some nights, I pray."

And Grandma, have you left the camps, the war?
I turned off the lamp, the guards closed my door.

GRAFFITI

On a toilet, in a locker room,
    I search walls for the dark side in ink,

find dirty talk above numbers
    of those I imagine dialing: Hal, the janitor

whose eyes trail down us like suds;
    Mr. Stanton, who suspends me twice

for smoking pot; and Mr. Gray, the gym teacher
    who models for Sears and autographs catalogs for girls.

With a dime, I scrape at whitewash,
    flake the shoes I pad to reach the height

of star quarterback, Chip Fuller.
    Tracing Julie's cheerleader breasts,

the outline of enormous nipples, I guess
    who wrote *Go team go* beneath her and Chip.

I suspect Chip came up with the slogan
    Joey Finley, four-eyed sissy who can't get

any KUNT. I hunt for the boys
    Chip mocks by raising his voice

soprano—*Boy George, Boytano, Burishnikoff, suck*
    my ballz—Billy Crescent in his tights, practicing pirouettes

for the next Nutcracker, and Joey each time he backs
    away from a pass. The buck-toothed, slit-eyed drawing

of my mother turns the joke on me.
    I fight to see the caption *Go home Jap bitch*

through the blue eyes of Chip,
    to know his touch for winning, praised

by a handshake from Mr. Stanton,
    a pat on the back from Mr. Gray.

The bold of felt-tips,
    our black and blue pains the room

where Hal pulls his mop over the floor
    while Chip and his teammates knead Ben-Gay

into stiff limbs, ease joints with ice and tape,
    envious as they listen to how Chip is going

to take Julie doggie style in his basement,
    or in the back of his father's car, hold her face

against anything that muffles the sound,
　　　her silence like Joey's, like Billy's, like my mother's,

even mine, our silence in the words I smear
　　　with the spit on my sleeve and begin to rub out.

UNCLE KUNI HOLDS IN TOPAZ

I am white-gloved, the pew varnished.
      Citrus fire from his mouth, burst vein
of our past. Is it then

      or now his mother pats his forehead with wet towels
and his sisters wring out the cloth? The ceiling

      of the ambulance shakes. My uncle Kuni wants air. I am
not there. The time I prodded him hard, he held
      everything in. *What camp? How long?* Tell

me. Fucking answer, I yelled in my head, mind ablaze
      after I left the church where he lived

and cared for his parents
      alone. The bitter taste of horsemeat
is why Kuni fevered, skinned his knees crawling for oranges

      white kids threw over the fence. More than seeds
of one story, I want to taste the grove's glow

      in his arid prison. I drove
fast, the grocery bag of history books he gave me
      jostling in the backseat. Wilted peels

at my uncle's feet, peach carnation petals scatter
      across his unrising

chest. A tipped over chair, his father dialed
    911. Trout bones. A shattered
plate. A hole in his heart. I have no prayer for distant fruit

    shrouded in leaves, broken fish out of streams. Everything spills
into the hospital. Glass doors release, orderlies rush

    out. White everywhere and sheets bright as floodlit
sand. My rage dissolved, washed out by his sad quiet. Every road I take
    leads us to orange memories.

                                        —for Kunimaro Ishida, 1936-1993

MEASURE

Uncle Kibi, did I come to see you as only half a man
with your shaved head and lead blanket,
half the weight, half the breath, half the smile,
only half of you looking at the doctor
who loaded up the transparency, used a ruler
to show the tumor, its increments,
this angle, 70%, that angle 50%, back at half
again, in this case, your chance of living.
1 set of x-rays needed, a 2nd opinion, a 3rd, each
arbitrary as the 4 vertebrae swarmed
by the 4,123 diseased cells, the 7,000
blood count, 5,126 swollen lymphs,
and the fact that there were 3 doctors,
6 orderlies, 9 interns only made calculations
trickier. 2 options: 48 weeks of radiation
or 12 hours under the knife. 3 pills a day
after either treatment. Within 1 year
a 50% chance to live. A 250,000
deductible to cover cost after the 8th week.
1 oxygen tank and cane for full recovery.
The 1 opaque streak vanishing from
the transparency. The 2 cigars we smoked
to celebrate. Our 1 hour tennis match,
the score 6-3 because you didn't want
any measure of pity, my 5 aces, your 4 double
faults, no strategy against the 3 opaque streaks
growing back into the transparency. The 29 steps

to your room where I tied the white laces
of your gown. The 1 tuna fish sandwich
I brought you Sunday, the 7th, at 8 p.m.,
2 bites while you looked out the window
at 2 sparrows darting back and forth, warbling
atop 1 branch, a single pine cone falling.

—for Kibimaro Ishida, 1944-1995

GATEKEEPER

Any noise alerts me. My wife Grace shifts beneath our comforter.
Respecting my uncles long dead, I climb from bed, grab
the bat, climb stairs, walk halls with a thousand sutras shelved
high, my grandparents' moonlit ink floating on pages sheer
as veils, the word *Love* rescued from censors. In the nursery
I check window-locks, sense my son Brendan falling in and out
of seizures and sleep. Backed by the altar, its purple chrysanthemum
curtains, gold-leafed lily pads, corroded rice paper, I crouch
then stand at the window to watch silhouettes fleeing
past streetlamps, the gate unmoored from its deadbolt, unhinged
from ill-fitted screws and rusted nails. The front door cottoned
with fog shakes in night wind. Backyard bushes rustle. For now
I let the mendicants crack open our prickly crowns of aloe, soothe
their faces with gel, drop bottle-shards and cigarette butts that slash
and burn our stairs. Inside, we fit apart and together.
Grace and Brendan sleeping, me standing guard.
From my grandfather's scrolls moths fly out, and I grab at air
to repel the strangeness of other lives circling toward us.

PEARL

Through temple windows
    I divide

the moon,
    half-Japanese,

half-white,
    a broken pearl

in the sky's
    dark harbor.

MY WIFE GRACE REFLECTS ON HER GREAT AUNT'S JADE

I.

I open the varnished box,
unwrap the necklace
you gave me
from crepe paper,
polish the jade triangle

until my fingerprints
are gone. I look
in the mirror at how alike
we are: my hair long
and dark like yours,

my skin the same olive shade.
On silver chain
your heirloom rests,
nestled in the V
of my collarbone.

II.

My husband Brian clasps
the gem on me, presses
his warm lips
to my neck, touching
my mole—a dot

on the map, your city, Nanking.
He is half as Japanese
as soldiers who sliced
you away.
Jade cannot soothe

or return you
nor cool
the pit of flame.
Moments before
their bootsteps,

III.

your kitchen was fragrant
with black bean and garlic,
the sweetness
of rice wine
on your husband's breath

as he unclasped
this jewel from your neck.
When my infant son, Brendan—
Cheung-Hong you'd call him—
pulls the jade

to his mouth,
he tastes you
in its swirling green.
Great Aunt,
we mark you in stone.

EXPOSURE

In the movie, a woman sits in front of a mirror,
watching her hair fall out.

My hand searches the bag between Amber's legs.

My fingertips are butter and salt when I lick them,
and when the camera pans to the right side of the woman's head,

I cringe at the single bald spot.

Is exposed flesh the reason she fiddles
with the lock of the varnished box?

The booth projects the beam

of my father's flashlight, leading us beneath
the porch, down a ladder, through a maze of pipes,

to an entrance where he clears away cobwebs.

And this woman is my mother captured by photos
after the war: in our church she is dressed in a *kimono*,

u-shaped pins propping her hair, her face powdered with talc.

Where is the key to unlock this box?
A bomb shelter my father calls it. Night after night

I climb under the covers while he descends

beneath the house, the tip of his shovel ticking
against the earth like a metronome.

And during the drills, when I crawl under my desk,

I turn to him, down on his hands and knees
as he tape measures length and depth, arranges

the brick into rows to trowel with mortar.

Our secret place he calls it. Amber and I
are hidden away like his jugs of water and boxes

of powdered eggs, the air black as a minister's frock.

Perhaps the cross beneath Amber's sweater
is why I harden alone inside my jeans, why I want

to unknot the sash of the woman on screen, to explore

each scar she soothes with aloe,
each blemish of my father who shucks off

his plaid shirt and boots while I peek through a crack in the door.

And the woman lifts the veil of hair, exposing
another bald spot; is she why I leave the theater,

turn away from Amber in some abandoned lot?

I've forgotten if the woman finds the clip
or if the box remains locked,

and whether this was my mother who used to sit

this same way, my father combing out her knots
with a pearl-handled brush.

The hairpin she picks up has a butterfly,

carved into silver, veined with chartreuse
and magenta. Now the naked patch

is the blank screen, and I think it's my father

who finds the delicate wing,
to draw back her hair's dark curtain.

THE CHAIN

You swaggered with the girls you'd done and the girls
you wanted to do, *the virgins, the sluts, the prudes*
with red hair and freckles, your cock
in a forest of orange, or the blonde goddess

who didn't know our first names, flicking back
her hair while she blew smoke rings between classes,
and me bragging how this weekend it would be me
with Amber, her cross and the chain I'd unclasp,

when she popped, the cherry stain, and after
I stuffed the sheet in the hamper, how sore she would be
when I left her in bed, her underwear on the post,
she'd wake without a note, without a phone call,

for you, Derek, I added her to our chain of names which grew
during gym class between glimpses at the boys
you called *flamers*, Billy Crescent who'd never know
how to mount the way we did, except the missionary,

and only with a boy, not with boys like us, how I shivered
to picture him, giving it or taking it, so convenient
to forget him, to block out my feigned belief
in Amber's Jesus who told her to wait, and we did,

but instead I was proud to lie to you, it seemed
I did have sex each week, each score another level
on *the food chain* you called it, each cliché
a variation on the last, *She went down on me so long*

she was gasping the lines we learned rewinding
the VCR in your basement where you laid newspaper
across your parents' rug, *For practice* you said,
to be the one who lasts, but I hoped I knew the real reason

our cocks were jackhammers in our Vaselined fists
side by side with a speaker between us, my hands
going up and down, an imagined mouth, first Amber's,
then Billy's, maybe the O of his lips slightly bigger,

maybe behind the cover of pines Billy's act
more secret, hurried, we were lost when
we came, unaware of your parents' key turning
in the front door, why didn't Billy hear the boys

in the park with chains around their fists,
the links which sent him to intensive care,
later in the auditorium the way you whispered *fairy*
into my ear and this time, I didn't turn my head

or nod, instead taking in Billy as he leapt
and spun across the stage, merged into the girls,
each movement soothing me, his eye
bruised dark as steel beneath the eye patch,

the flesh lashed red beneath his tights,
his grace hiding the remnants of violence, ·
your scoff when I told you I would face Amber,
and when I did, it was much different,

something about commitment to God, being true
to her too, my white lie like a sin straight
to her face, beneath the blanket, how she was
the first and only one I would ever make love to,

even as the others began to blur into me, ready
to pretend she was them, or not them at all, only a glimmer
of you and the gang of boys as her cross dangled
above my mouth, linking her to me, shifting the chain.

BEFORE

Son, Hiroshima fragments were gone
        before I could ask your
great-grandfather Ojichan about
        his farm, where chickens smelled
of cherry blossoms
        before the button inside the plane

clocks ticked
           in rooms
      shades of light
             filtered

through windows
          parents stood
      at barn doors
             telephone poles buzzed

with words
        still spoken.

ORIGIN

Through darkness they came,
       covered in ash, scarred by depths

and distance, they bore salt and fire, breath steaming
       at edges of decks, hands clutching

railings, their bodies dizzied by the lurching vessel,

       trunks pulled by hand, *Where are you from?* I unwrapped
my legacy from cloth, the marble Buddha

       from my grandfather, ancient
as the sea-stained covers of his sutras, the briny odor

       of carp centuries old. *What are you?*

Not only where they were from but who they were
       and would become. His strange

past and the mystery of my own face, *American?*
       this question flawed as we all

appeared, my grandfather's birthplace the half of me

       I lightened, bleaching my black hair
to reach my girlfriend Amber's blonde.

In her candlelit room, I touched
the mission photo of her

rubbing ointment on the burns

of a *hibakusha. Where are*
water-filled troughs and the horses' manes

my grandfather combed. The hay he bundled
in twine. *you from?* Could he have smoothed names

engraved in granite, the scars on the woman's skin, targets

raised on maps? In a light blast *What are* a city
of *nips* was erased. *you?* A blank scape, *Go back*

no trace of his childhood farm
in Hiroshima, *to where* I turned

away from the chalkboard scrawled

with Enola Gay, *you are* a button pushed,
from a bomb dropped, at Amber's picnic

they bowed over grace, and I looked up, didn't
say Amen. Everything rises

when the ground's skin is broken.

WILLIAM L. LAURENCE, JOURNALIST ON THE PLANE THAT BOMBED NAGASAKI, YEARS LATER IN BED WITH HIS WIFE

Moving forward
or back? Which way

am I? I wake grasping

your nightgown.
I am still

there. In the haze of faces

burning. Arch
of spreading

flame, black-haired girl

in saddle shoes
and plaid skirt, knee-deep

in a yard of violets.

Her father, in clogs, pounding a path
home, balancing

buckets of carp

on a bamboo pole.
Daughter, father, splash

of carp, magenta rows,

white light's flashbulb zing
fades as I cling

to silk's edge, slats

of ribs
a bridge I take

to your belly's bulge.

My pollen inside you, nubs
of arms and legs, hands with fingers

petaling. Vase of roses on the night stand.

Your gold ring engraved
with my initials. The father, feet

from the gate, his daughter

kneeling with shears,
pruning flowerbeds.

Sealed in sheets,

I draw close
to your body,

place my ear against flesh,

listen to the rhythmic thumping
inside water.

BLACK SKY

—Hiroshima, 1945

The flash so fast, it catches me here. In the frame of a window
looking out. A blur of spokes, you are getting close, pedaling
hard, bamboo basket brimming with peaches. Behind you
the orchard, your ladder, swept up in flame. High in branches,
you had picked *momo* as I steadied you below, your shirt billowing,
carrying the scent of sugar and salt. The basket nearing full,
I walked the path home. I washed the fruit bowl well, waiting
for your return, and the soap foam dissolved into water.

These moments take no time. The dust plume of your bicycle,
wheels spinning too slow to escape lilacs that burn. The black sky
captures us: inked words, stains on my white apron, strings
untied. You knew ripeness by touch, one hand tracing
my hip in the steaming *furo*. All of this singed with nectar.
A grove of ash, blackened leaves through windows,
the roof consumed.

We reach through scorched wall,
light filling us,
our bodies of fallen snow.

MY GRANDMOTHER'S KITCHEN

She is the poem
    left behind, the silence
of white space

breathing between
    the dark characters,
steady as the legs

of the oak desk
    where her ink settles to dry
on paper. She opens

a window to our church,
    leans out to reel in underwear
and shirts, unclip

the pins, folds the clothes
    into stacks precise as the lines
she builds from syllables.

For husband, sons, and daughters,
    she measures hunger in eight spoons,
eight bowls, eight cups, forgetting

her place in the count,
        her flow of words drowned out
by the hissing kettle

she lifts from the stove.
        While the children thirst for
the weight of her ladle,

cubes of tofu bobbing
        in miso broth, she withdraws
to the nibbed tip of her pen,

its fountain pulling her
        back to Ito, foam breaking
over sharpened rocks

where Saint Nichiren landed,
        the *tatami* room where she was born.
Her rhythm and pause

are caught in the dulled
        teeth of a rusted knife,
the scuffed slate

of cutting boards,
        in the walls of this pot, burnished
by the burner's blue hiss.

Like these things
        she grows unnoticed,
a haiku among recipes.

—for Chiyoko Saito Ishida, 1905-1993

MORNING SUTRA

Grandmother is
dreaming me
into my uncles
while I read
the violet sutra,
sponging her forehead
with a hot cloth.
Each presses her
petal dress,
soaps the gold
from her finger,
pulls the needle
from her frayed vein
as her face slackens
into the quiet lid
of a closed box.
But they left
this temple bedroom
long ago,
so I pretend
to be them for her
finding the roundness
in her face,
knowing her breath
will come.

JACKET ELEGY

It was found in a snowy field, tangled in pines,

attached to the cables of your parachute.
The night my lover runs from her father

I drape it over her, place an ice pack against her head.

I trace the grooves of the eagle
in each brass button, the silver-winged patches of your jacket

that guided you through Pyongyang sky.

Your landing is revealed
in the stitch and weave of the torn lining,

the tangled net of branches bending

to your weight. Inside the steaming forest
of needles and cones,

I summon you, your coat heavy and cold

as the bag of ice that numbs us
from the strike of his hand,

your hands gnarled from striking stones

until they sparked. In your heat
her shivers grow quiet, fade out

like her bruise into the roots of hair.

I watch for you in the flare
rising out of her father's headlights

through my blinds, the footprints he leaves

stalking us through snow.
While he burns a circle

to see through each window of my house,

I hold her close inside the twilled fabric,
your tattered nest of blue wool.

Uncle, do you stray between the cover of trees

and the iced banks of a river,
the way she wavers

between me and her father's home?

Leave him were his words in Korean
as he dragged her across the floor

by the hair. *Stay* I whisper

in her ear until her lumps subside—
the bag of ice turns to water, to the melted snow

you drank from your cupped hands.

Uncle Hide, when you return to us,
take cover in the changing shape of your coat,

our refuge of mothballs and guava perfume.

—for Hidemaro Ishida, 1932-MIA, Korean War, 1953

CLOUD

I bow to your fallen sons *Hidemaro, Kunimaro, Kibimaro*
    scrolled bold against blank, made
monumental by *sumi* from your brush. I change water

    from cloudy to clear, gladioli
open inside porcelain, nectar of old Hiroshima. Spring breezes
    on your parents' farm, you galloped

across green. Now, Grandfather, you look through me, mind
    billowing, our names and birthdates
vaporized like your childhood inside a hot wind. I meld

    with Uncle Kazu and Aunt Tae into one
form, and our church becomes, for you, a specter of buried
    hoofprints and singed clover.

BEADS

Smooth against

    my skin,

        a long strand passes

    through us

to Brendan, my son.

MIGRATION

Some mornings are braided with wingbeats
of rain, the flap of peeling wallpaper, the mildewed must

of the church I return to.

The creak of spindles wakes me from dreams
of everyone cold and faraway. In the crib

where my mother once slept,

my son Brendan, shivering, babbles his syllabic call.
To quiet my mother's cries, her parents drew their bodies

out of the sagging nest my wife and I now climb from,

folding back the sheets
like wings, the memory of their flight

inside our feet as we gather our son, glide him through hallways.

Their comings and goings are real and far
as rainfall and trains inside the temple bell, a hawk's circlings.

Though we follow their current, we find our own way—

to the kitchen where I ignite the furnace,
where Brendan closes his lips around Grace's nipple,

suckles himself to sleep.

To bring my wife and son peace,
I would travel miles toward the doorbell's chime

and its shrill persistence.

In the smudged globe
of the peephole,

a homeless woman looms out of proportion.

If I journey the foreign *kanji* of Grandfather's scrolls,
the veiled meaning of the crazy's mantra becomes clear:

I am Buddha . . . the second Coming . . . This is my house of God . . .

Prayer is the flower in rain, its drops falling
on the roof of this church

where Grace fills a plastic tub warm for Brendan.

Prayer softens the parched ground,
my grandfather kneeling to a fallen hawk

at the foot of a guard tower, wings thrashing

the way Brendan's arms do
while his mother Grace holds him afloat.

Something caged flutters inside the past:

Grandmother and her children were taken
from our church, Grandfather barracked miles away

when they, like him, were tagged and numbered.

Only when I circle back, can I continue beyond:
to my wife Grace, who swaddles Brendan in a towel;

this vagrant woman on the porch whose coat spans

into wings, each bruise and scar on her ribs,
the battered body of the hawk.

As she buttons herself up, I warm

to the pain concealed beneath any coat,
the hope of it lifting away

like the hawk from my grandfather,

how he lightened after he boarded the freight,
the miles of track slatted like the banister winding me up

stairs to Grace cradling Brendan, my lips burning

into hers, a church of rain,
the train's steam rising off Brendan's skin,

the flight of years reaching destination

when my grandmother touched
my grandfather's bearded face,

and my infant mother returned to him

quieted, like our son,
a plum inside my cupped hands.

OVER THE EARTH

—Nanking, 1937

I don't want us
to end here, wondering
who will be first,

our eyes lowered
as the soldiers raise
their blades,

slicing those
ahead of us.
Kneeling by the gutter,

I conjure our home
in fading light.
At the kitchen table

you opened
a bottle of plum wine,
unwrapped paper,

lifted the vein
to filet soft meat.
Now their swords strike

closer, the ground shifts
with each head cut
from its stem,

I hear the thud
of your rolling pin
pounding flour,

the dust rising
like bone smoke.
The edge is near, my love.

Skies darken
into our room,
the clouds a line

of ivory buttons
on the blue silk
of your dress.

NOTES

In this manuscript, the church and temple refer to the Nichiren Buddhist Church of America in San Francisco that my late grandfather, Archbishop Nitten Ishida, founded in 1931. He and his family lived there before and after they were incarcerated in prison camps—along with over one-hundred and twenty thousand other Japanese Americans—from 1942-1946.

Separated from wife and children and detained in various internment camps, my grandfather, a Buddhist priest and calligrapher, turned to prayer and painting in order to cope with his anxieties about his family's well-being during the war. Meanwhile, my grandmother cared for their children, including my infant mother Renko, in Topaz concentration camp, officially known as Central Utah Relocation Center. The family ultimately reunited in Crystal City Internment Camp in Texas. Later, they found their way back to the church—their former home ravaged by boarders and vandals—where they attempted to rebuild their lives.

"Crossing" is for Garrett Hongo, Richard Tillinghast, Jill Allyn Rosser, Anastasia Royal, and the entire Ishida family.

"Sugar" is for Edward Hirsch, who suggested the trope of sweetness for this poem, and for Li-Young Lee.

"I Factor in My Mother's Division from Her Father with a Sentence Written by Lieutenant General John L. DeWitt in 1942" was first inspired by Josie Kearns and is for her. The quote from John L. DeWitt and numbers used in the poem are taken from p. 82 and p. 88 of *Personal Justice Denied*; this quote also appears on p. 110 of *Prejudice, War, and the*

Constitution by Jacobus tenBroek, Edward N. Barnhart, and Floyd W. Matson, University of California Press, 1954.

"A Conversation with My Mother, Renko, About the Journey to and from Topaz Prison Camp in a Dream" owes a debt of influence to David St. John's "Iris" and Li-Young Lee's "This Room and Everything in It."

"Temple Bell Lesson" is for Brendan.

Parts of "Transaction" are informed by the compelling documentary *Who Killed Vincent Chin?* by Christine Choy and Renee Tajima.

Helpful sources in my writing of "The Strip" include C.K. Williams' "The Gas Station" and Paul Monette's *Borrowed Time: An AIDS Memoir.*

In "Admission," *Namu Myōhō Renge Kyō* translates to *The Sutra of the Lotus Flower of the Wonderful Law,* and *Ren* means "lotus," which is the prefix in my mother's name, Renko. The Nichiren sect of Buddhism, founded by Saint Nichiren and practiced by my late grandfather, uses *The Lotus Sutra* as its primary spiritual text.

"Chandelier" is for Grace.

The initial impetus for writing "Winter Letter to San Francisco" came from my reading of wartime family letters and David Mura's "Letters from Poston Relocation Camp (1942-45)." The references to breaking records, folding the flag, and discarding other Japanese cultural markers underscore the tremendous pressure Japanese Americans felt—due to wartime hysteria, racism, and governmental policy—to hide their Japanese heritage and to display their loyalty to America.

Intergenerational silence is a motif in the literature and poetry of Japanese Americans about the incarceration during World War II. "My Questions to Obachan, Her Answers" owes a debt to David Mura and is for him. Particular sources of inspiration are Mura's "An Argument: On 1942" and Joy Kogawa's *Obasan*. In line 11, the decision to answer "yes" refers to question 27 of the Loyalty Questionnaire, which asked Japanese American camp prisoners if they were willing to serve in the US Armed Forces.

"Graffiti" shows the influence of Timothy Liu. His collections *Vox Angelica* and *Burnt Offerings* have been inspiring.

"Measure" is dedicated to Deborah, Rebecca, and Keith.

"My Wife Grace Reflects on Her Great Aunt's Jade" is based on the history of my wife Grace's great grandfather's third wife—her family was killed by the Japanese in Nanking in 1937.

The film referred to in "Exposure" is *Black Rain* (*Kuroi Ame*), directed by Shohei Imamura (1989).

"William L. Laurence, Journalist on the Plane That Bombed Nagasaki, Years Later in Bed with His Wife" was written in response to William L. Laurence's "Atomic Bombing of Nagasaki Told by Flight Member," which appears in *Fields of Reading* edited by Nancy Comley et al. (Bedford/St. Martin's, 2007). According to this source, Laurence "won the Pulitzer prize for this account" which "appeared in the *New York Times* on September 9, 1945."

"Beads" and other poems refer to the Buddhist rosary or *juzu*. The 108 beads are divided in two sections of 54 each, representing the 54 stages of becoming a bodhisattva. As a whole, the beads symbolize the path to enlightenment and oneness of all life.

"Migration" is for Grace, Brendan, my parents Stuart and Renko, brother Loren, aunts Tae and Nori, and uncle Kazu.

"Over the Earth" is dedicated to the memory of Iris Chang (1968-2004). The powerful images and stories from her book, *The Rape of Nanking: The Forgotten Holocaust of World War II*, were helpful in the writing of this poem.

ACKNOWLEDGMENTS

Grateful acknowledgment is made to the editors of the following publications where these poems first appeared, some of them in earlier versions and with modified titles:

The Asian Pacific American Journal, Bellingham Review, Beloit Poetry Journal, Crab Orchard Review, Green Mountains Review, Gulf Coast, Many Mountains Moving, The Massachusetts Review, New England Review, North American Review, Parthenon West Review, Ploughshares, Post Road, Prairie Schooner, Quarterly West, River Styx.

"Measure" appeared in *BigCityLit.com.*

"Transaction" appeared in *Screaming Monkeys: Critiques of Asian American Images* edited by M. Evelina Galang (Coffee House Press, 2003).

"Measure" and "Exposure" appeared in *Asian American Poetry: The Next Generation* edited by Victoria Chang (University of Illinois Press, 2004).

"Your Hands Guide Me Through Trains" appeared in *Language for a New Century: Contemporary Poetry from the Middle East, Asia, and Beyond* edited by Tina Chang, Nathalie Handal, and Ravi Shankar (W.W. Norton & Co., 2008).

"Spring Reply to Internment Camp, Location Unknown" appeared in *A Face to Meet the Faces: An Anthology of Contemporary Persona Poetry* edited by Stacey Lynn Brown and Oliver de la Paz (The University of Akron Press, 2012).

"Sickness" appeared in *Green Mountains Review: 25th Anniversary Poetry Retrospective* (2012).

"Transaction" was nominated by *The Asian Pacific American Journal* for a Pushcart Prize and "Sugar" was a finalist for the Lucille Medwick Memorial Award (2001) of the Poetry Society of America. Various poems in this manuscript were finalists for the Alice Fay Di Castagnola Award (2005) and the George Bogin Memorial Award (2005, 2010) of the Poetry Society of America.

In the long road to completion of this book, I am grateful to many teachers who guided me along the way. I offer my deepest thanks to Garrett Hongo and Richard Tillinghast for their longtime friendship, wise mentorship, and unwavering support. A further debt is owed to Jill Allyn Rosser for her kindness, insight, and belief in my work. Edward Hirsch, Li-Young Lee, and David Mura also deserve recognition for their significant role in my poetic development and encouragement of my creative vision. Special thanks go out to Joan Houlihan and the Colrain Poetry Manuscript Conference for thoughtful readings of the manuscript in its later stages; to Michael Collier, Jennifer Grotz, Noreen Cargill and the Bread Loaf Writers' Conference for numerous opportunities to experience artistic communion and growth; and to Martha Rhodes for her warmth, vision, and attentiveness. Additional credit is due to the staff at Four Way Books for their skill and dedication: Sally Ball, Bridget Bell, Victoria McCoy, and Ryan Murphy.

Various friends and writing communities were instrumental to the evolution of this work as well. I express gratitude to Anastasia Royal for her close friendship and generous, brilliant editing. Over the last decade, her depth of commitment to my work and understanding of my aesthetic have been essential to the realization of this book. Friends Brenda Cárdenas, Tina Chang, Patrick Phillips, and Glori Simmons offered insightful and intensive readings as well. Past and present members of the Seventeen Syllables Collective—Sabina Chen, Edmond Chow, Jay Dayrit, Lillian Howan, Roy Kamada, Caroline Kim, Suji Kwock Kim, Grace Loh Prasad, and Marianne Villanueva—were pillars of sustenance. The Poet's Choice crew infused me with further courage and inspiration: Dean Rader, Chris Haven, Katie Cappello, Brian Clements, Amorak Huey, Todd Kaneko, Amy McInnis, Christina Olson, Jean Prokott, and Mark Schaub. I am grateful to the Royal-Ingram clan, a family that lives and breathes poetry; thanks for their insights about mine. The writers of *From Our Side of the Fence* and *Making Home from War* educated and inspired me with their powerful stories of wartime incarceration and post-war resettlement. Jason Chu, Rodolfo del Rosario Victoria, Estevan Rael-Gálvez, Dard Neuman, Eric Nikaido, Steven Salchak, David Shih, James Tjoa, and Marc Wallis were brothers in spirit who carried me through the journey.

Moreover, gratitude is due to organizations that provided me with crucial time and support. I am indebted to the Arts Foundation of Michigan and Michigan Council for Arts and Cultural Affairs for a Creative Artist Grant that aided me in the development of this manuscript. I am also grateful to the Ragdale Foundation, Ucross Foundation, Vermont Studio Center, and Villa Montalvo for residency fellowships and University of San Francisco Faculty Development Fund for valuable assistance.

Finally, I feel blessed for the love of my wife Grace, son Brendan, parents Stuart and Renko, brother Loren, and the Chow family—Lok, Chi-Ieng, and Candace—who supported me during the many years of writing this book. My deceased grandfather's church—the Nichiren Buddhist Church of America—gave me sacred hours, space, and inspiration for many of these poems. Love goes out to Aunt Tae for her tenderness and knowledge of our family history; to Aunt Nori and Uncle Kazu for their caring ways; to them and the extended Ishida family for their kinship; and to the living spirits for whom these pages are dedicated.

Brian Komei Dempster is editor of both *From Our Side of the Fence: Growing Up in America's Concentration Camps* (Kearny Street Workshop, 2001), which received a 2007 Nisei Voices Award from the National Japanese American Historical Society, and *Making Home from War: Stories of Japanese American Exile and Resettlement* (Heyday, 2011). His poems have been published in *New England Review, North American Review*, and *Ploughshares*, and the anthologies *Language for a New Century: Contemporary Poetry from the Middle East, Asia, and Beyond* (Norton, 2008) and *Asian American Poetry: The Next Generation* (University of Illinois, 2004). His work—as a poet, workshop instructor, and editor—has been recognized by grants from the Arts Foundation of Michigan and the Michigan Council for Arts and Cultural Affairs, the California State Library's California Civil Liberties Public Education Program, the Center for Cultural Innovation, and the San Francisco Arts Commission. Dempster has also received scholarships to the Bread Loaf Writers' Conference. He is a professor of rhetoric and language and a faculty member in Asian Pacific American Studies at the University of San Francisco. *Topaz* is his debut book of poetry.